Voices of the CIVIL WAR

STORIES FROM THE BATTLEFIELDS

by Jason D. Nemeth

Consultant:
Mark A. Snell, PhD
Associate Professor of History/Director
George Tyler Moore Center for the Study of the Civil War
Shepherd University
Shepherdstown, West Virginia

CAPSTONE PRESS
a capstone imprint

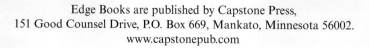

Edge Books are published by Capstone Press,
151 Good Counsel Drive, P.O. Box 669, Mankato, Minnesota 56002.
www.capstonepub.com

 Books published by Capstone Press are manufactured with paper
containing at least 10 percent post-consumer waste.

Library of Congress Cataloging-in-Publication Data
Nemeth, Jason D.
 Voices of the Civil War : stories from the battlefields / by Jason Nemeth.
   p. cm. — (Edge books. Voices of war)
 Summary: "Describes first-hand accounts of the Civil War from those who lived
   through it"—Provided by publisher.
 Includes bibliographical references and index.
 ISBN 978-1-4296-4736-6 (library binding)
 ISBN 978-1-4296-5625-2 (paperback)
 1. United States—History—Civil War, 1861–1865—Biography—Juvenile
   literature. I. Title. II. Series.
 E467.N46 2011
 973.7092'2—dc22   2010006604

Editorial Credits
Kathryn Clay, editor; Tracy Davies, designer; Svetlana Zhurkin,
   media researcher; Laura Manthe, production specialist

Photo Credits
Getty Images/Kean Collection, 28; Getty Images/MPI, 14; Getty Images/Stock
Montage, 17; Library of Congress, cover (top), cover (letter), 7, 9, 12–13, 18, 19, 21, 22,
23, 26 (top), 26–27; North Wind Picture Archives, 6, 8, 15, 24 (bottom); Shutterstock/
Adam Tinney (flames), cover, back cover, 1; Shutterstock/Ann Triling (stars),
throughout; Shutterstock/Benjamin F. Haith (U.S. flag), cover; Shutterstock/Cagri Oner
(torn paper), throughout; Shutterstock/Igorsky (stone wall), 9, 17, 21; Shutterstock/
kzww (rusty background), throughout; Shutterstock/Lora Liu (paper background),
throughout; Shutterstock/Mark R (smoke), cover, back cover, 1; Shutterstock/Matt
Trommer (Confederate flag), cover; Shutterstock/Vladislav Gajic (cannon), cover; U.S.
Naval Historical Center/NARA, 11; U.S. Naval Historical Center/New Jersey Historical
Society, 10; Wikipedia, 24 (top); XNR Productions (map), 5

TABLE OF CONTENTS

1 A NATION DIVIDED

In the early morning of April 12, 1861, a shot was fired over the harbor in Charleston, South Carolina. This was the signal to other **Confederate** soldiers to begin the bombardment on **Union** soldiers at Fort Sumter. With a single shot, America's bloodiest conflict had begun.

Americans had long disagreed about slavery. Many people in the northern states were against owning slaves. In the South, slaves were considered property. Wealthy plantation owners wanted slaves to harvest their crops.

When Abraham Lincoln was elected president in November 1860, many southerners feared he would end slavery. Southerners also argued that individual states didn't have enough power in government. Some states decided to form their own country, the Confederate States of America. In December 1860, South Carolina became the first state to **secede**. Mississippi, Florida, Alabama, Georgia, Texas, and Louisiana soon followed.

Confederate: having to do with the southern states that formed the Confederate States of America

secede: to formally withdraw from a group or an organization

Union: the states that remained loyal to the federal government during the Civil War

Confederate soldiers demanded the surrender of Union soldiers at Fort Sumter, South Carolina. When the Union didn't, the Confederate army took the fort by force. Soon after, Virginia, Arkansas, Tennessee, and North Carolina joined the Confederacy. The rest of the states remained part of the Union. But the split wasn't easy. Some people in the North supported the Confederacy. Some people in the South fought for the Union.

Everyone had a different reason for fighting. Some fought out of loyalty to their state. Others wanted to protect the Union. Later in the war, people fought to end slavery and become equal citizens. Here are some of the stories of the people who lived through it all.

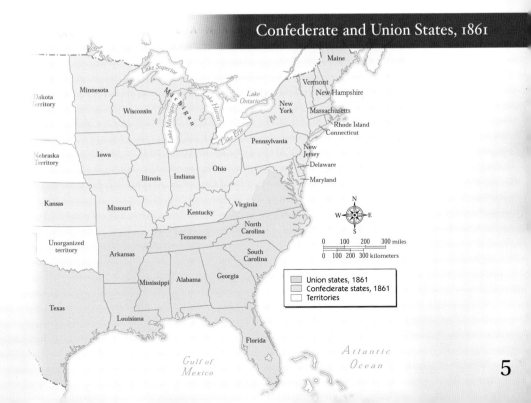

Confederate and Union States, 1861

2

SAM WATKINS: CONFEDERATE SOLDIER

a Confederate soldier

Sam Watkins was 21 years old when he joined the First Tennessee **Infantry** in 1861. While training at Camp Cheatham, Watkins dreamed about how he would bravely face the enemy. He was excited by the adventure of war and the chance to support the Confederacy.

A LONG WAIT

Despite his excitement for battle, Watkins didn't see action for nearly a year. Instead, he marched with other soldiers from one camp to another. They walked so much that the skin on Watkins' feet peeled off like the layers of an onion.

infantry: a group of soldiers trained to fight and travel on foot

When they weren't marching, the soldiers stayed in camp. But camp life was boring. Watkins and the other soldiers made up games to pass the time. One game was louse racing. The men picked lice off their bodies and put them on a plate. Whichever louse ran off the plate first was the winner.

Even without battle, marching and camping could be dangerous for the soldiers. In January 1862, temperatures were so cold that soldiers froze to death. "Some were sitting down and some were lying down," Watkins said. "But each and every one was as cold and as hard frozen as the icicles that hung from their hands and faces and clothing—dead!"

Confederate soldiers at camp

THE REALITY OF BATTLE

When battle finally arrived, it was not the great adventure Watkins had hoped for. One of the worst fights was the Battle of Perryville in Kentucky. Cannonballs crashed to the ground. Bullets tore through the air. Raging fires sent up smoke that clogged the soldiers' lungs.

Watkins' regiment began with about 1,200 men. When the men surrendered four years later on April 26, 1865, only 65 men had survived. Watkins was one of the lucky survivors who made it back to Tennessee.

The Battle of Perryville was fought on October 8, 1862.

young musicians ready for battle

Boys in the Civil War

Many soldiers in the Civil War were just boys. As long as they looked 18 years old and could pass a physical exam, they were allowed to join. Thousands of soldiers were under 16 years old.

Young boys who did not look old enough could join the army as musicians. Being a musician was not just a ceremonial role. Buglers and drummers marched into battle with the troops.

HENRY GUSLEY: UNION MARINE

3

USS *Westfield*

Henry Gusley loved books and poetry. He enjoyed them so much that he opened his own print shop in Lancaster, Pennsylvania. But when the war started, he left his shop to fight as a Union marine. Gusley was assigned to the USS *Westfield*. In October 1862, at age 24, he set sail from New York for the Gulf of Mexico.

STORMY WATERS

Gusley enjoyed sailing. His first few days at sea were peaceful. But one night a powerful ocean storm kicked up. Huge waves crashed over the ship, rocking it back and forth. The sailors and marines couldn't stand up without being knocked over. Anyone who dared to go up on deck would have been washed out to sea. When the storm passed, the ship was 100 miles (161 kilometers) off course.

A few days later, a second storm damaged the USS *Westfield*. Decking was ripped off by the strong winds. Parts of the ship filled with water. The ship didn't sink, but it had to be docked for a week so the damage could be repaired. Eventually, Gusley and the rest of the crew made it into the Gulf of Mexico.

aboard a Civil War gunboat

ENTERING THE MISSISSIPPI

Gusley entered the Mississippi River near New Orleans. The Union wanted to capture the southern city. The nearby river provided the Confederate army with access to troops and supplies. To attack from the water, Union ships had to get past Fort Jackson and Fort St. Philip.

Gusley and the rest of the crew helped defeat these forts. They camouflaged their ship with mud and branches. Then they snuck up with other Union ships and attacked the unsuspecting enemies.

vessels attacking near Fort Jackson

During these great battles, the air was thick with smoke. Cannon blasts shook the vessels. Shells whistled through the air and exploded like fireworks over their targets. More than 1,800 tons (1,600 metric tons) of **artillery** shells were fired by Union sailors and marines. After successfully taking both forts, Union ships moved upriver and captured New Orleans.

In September 1863, Gusley's ship was sunk, and he was taken prisoner. He spent 18 months in a Confederate prison camp before being released in 1865.

artillery: cannons and other large guns used during battles

4 THOMAS FANNING WOOD: CONFEDERATE DOCTOR

Moore Hospital

Thomas Fanning Wood was raised in Wilmington, North Carolina. He wanted to be a doctor when he grew up. But a lack of money stopped Wood from doing what he loved. Instead he had to work to help his family. But when the Civil War broke out, Wood was given a surprise chance to follow his dream.

FORT FISHER

Wood's father supported the Union. But Wood decided to fight for the 18th North Carolina Regiment of the Confederacy. In 1861, he and a group of young men he had grown up with trained at Fort Fisher, just south of Wilmington.

Wood and his friends treated camp life like a big vacation. Instead of preparing for war, they spent their days fishing, shooting marbles, or playing cards. They also spent time playing practical jokes on one another.

But it wasn't all fun and games. The men had responsibilities too. One of Wood's jobs was to make breakfast for the other soldiers. Wood wasn't a very good cook. When he tried to make biscuits, he couldn't get the dough to stick together. When he put his crumbly dough in the oven, the biscuits burned to a crisp. After that, Wood stayed away from the kitchen.

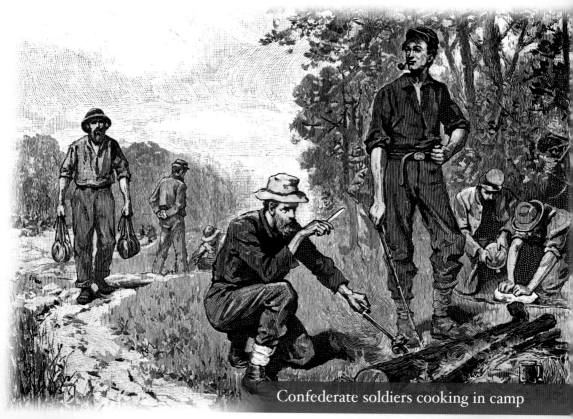

Confederate soldiers cooking in camp

A DREAM JOB

Wood saw only one battle during his first year as a soldier. Later he became feverish and went to Moore Hospital in Richmond, Virginia. The hospital was full of wounded soldiers, and there weren't enough doctors to treat them. When a doctor learned about Wood's interest in medicine, he put Wood in charge of 50 patients.

Wood was happy to be working in medicine, but he worried about being away from the battlefield. Because of the doctor shortage, the army let him continue working in the hospital. In January 1863, he passed the state's medical exam and became a doctor.

One month later, Wood was ordered to return to the battlefront. Wood's job was to follow behind and bandage the wounded. But at the Battle of Chancellorsville he was called to the field hospital. A soldier required an arm **amputation**. Wood had never done one before, but he picked up a saw and did his best.

Field doctors had few supplies. Wood noted how they used dirty sponges "over and over again ... infesting the wounded with each other's poison." Germs spread, making patients even sicker. After the war, Wood fought for better public health. He used what he learned on the battlefield to teach the importance of cleanliness.

Wounded soldiers were carried off the battlefield.

amputation: the removal of an arm or leg, usually because the part is damaged

Deadly Diseases

Disease and illness were serious problems during the Civil War. Sickness actually killed more soldiers than battlefield injuries. Almost 45,000 Union soldiers died from diarrhea caused by dysentery. Soldiers also suffered from malaria, pneumonia, and infections.

Many doctors were poorly trained or lacked proper equipment. Reusing dirty equipment spread germs from patient to patient. More than 600,000 men died during the war. Nearly 400,000 of these deaths were from illness.

5 WESLEY BRAINERD: UNION COLONEL

U.S. engineers in Virginia

As a young man, Wesley Brainerd wanted to study at the United States Military Academy at West Point, New York. Instead, he became an engineer. When the Civil War broke out, Brainerd finally got a chance to serve in the military. The decision wasn't easy. He had a wife and young daughter at home. He didn't want to leave them behind. But when the Union troops lost the Battle of Bull Run in July 1861, President Lincoln needed more troops. Brainerd and 18 other engineers formed a company and went to war.

BUILDING BRIDGES

Brainerd was in charge of the 50th New York Volunteer Engineers. They were trained as soldiers, but their main job was construction.

The unit built bridges so other troops could cross rivers and attack enemies. To build a bridge, the men spent many hours on the water. Mosquitoes, ticks, and snakes surrounded them. In fast-moving rivers, men could get swept away by the current. Sometimes they even had to build bridges in the middle of battles.

a pontoon bridge in Petersburg, Virginia, 1865

DODGING BULLETS

On December 10, 1862, Brainerd received orders to build a 400-foot (122-meter) bridge across the Rappahannock River. The location was in plain sight of Fredericksburg, Virginia, an enemy-held town. Brainerd believed the Confederate soldiers would see them coming. But because it was his duty as a soldier, he obeyed the order. Before starting the bridge, Brainerd wrote a farewell letter to his father.

Brainerd and his men began building just after midnight on December 11. In two hours they had finished half the bridge. But Confederate troops were starting to gather on the far shore. One hour later, the battle began. Bullets rained down on the bridge as Brainerd's men ran to shore. There was no protection on land. The men lay in the mud while bullets whizzed over their heads.

At 7:00 a.m. Brainerd was ordered to try building again. Despite sharpshooters on the other side, he took 10 men back to the bridge. Everyone was shot down in seconds. Brainerd was shot through the arm and barely made it off the bridge. Later, Union soldiers were able to chase away the Confederates and finish the bridge.

Union soldiers fought along the Rappahannock River in Virginia.

Civil War Food

A Union soldier's diet didn't have much variety. Soldiers received dried meat, sugar, coffee, and sometimes dried or fresh vegetables. They also ate thick crackers called hardtack. Hardtack was shipped to the battlefield in crates. When it reached the soldiers, it was usually stale and filled with worms. Instead of eating hardtack, Confederate soldiers cooked cornmeal into a dish called johnny cakes.

When soldiers headed on long marches, they took enough food for three days. Once Colonel Brainerd got called to march and had no time to pack food. He ate wormy hardtack and picked green corn and peaches along the way.

6 COLONEL JOHN MOSBY: CONFEDERATE RANGER

John Mosby did not lead a regular unit. His men were called partisan rangers. Their job was to raid Union camps, capture supply wagons, and cut telegraph lines. They attacked by surprise and disappeared quickly. Because he was so hard to catch, Mosby became known as the Gray Ghost.

Before the war, Mosby was a Virginia lawyer. He didn't want his state to secede from the Union. But when it did, he felt it was his duty to fight. Mosby started out as a private in the First Virginia Cavalry Regiment. His leadership skills stood out, and Mosby's commanders recognized his talents. They gave him his own unit to lead, the 43rd Battalion, Virginia Cavalry.

ENEMY RAID

Mosby liked to take chances. One time he snuck into a Union camp in the middle of the night. He brought only 29 men even though there were hundreds of Union soldiers surrounding them. Mosby walked into the enemy general's bedroom while he slept. He slapped the general on the back and ordered him to wake up. Without a gunshot ever being fired, Mosby and his men escaped with the general as their prisoner. This daring and dangerous raid made Mosby famous.

Even though the Confederacy lost the war, Mosby's men never officially surrendered. Too proud to admit defeat, they simply went back to their homes.

Mosby's men in the Shenandoah Valley

7 SUSIE KING TAYLOR: FREED SLAVE

Learning to read was dangerous for Susie King Taylor. As a young slave girl in Savannah, Georgia, she wasn't allowed to attend school. Anyone who tried to educate her would be considered a criminal. But that didn't stop people from trying.

When the Civil War broke out, Union troops took control of St. Simon's Island near Savannah. Many slaves fled there to be protected. Taylor went too. A Union navy officer learned of Taylor's education. He asked her to teach the freed slave children. She agreed, and the classroom quickly filled up with more than 40 children. Even a few adults joined the lessons.

But soon a regiment of black soldiers was formed to fight for the Union. Taylor's husband, Edward King, was a soldier in the United States Colored Troops. When he left for Jacksonville, Florida, Taylor went with him. While she was there, the Confederate army bombed the city. "I expected every moment to be killed by a shell," Taylor said. But she wasn't defenseless. While traveling with the regiment, Taylor helped clean and load the soldiers' guns. She learned how to take apart a musket and put it back together again. And she became a pretty good shooter.

When her husband was later stationed in South Carolina, Taylor crossed the Charleston Harbor to visit Fort Wagner. Skeletons of soldiers killed in earlier battles lay on the beach below the fort.

FREE AT LAST

Taylor lived to see the end of the war and freedom for slaves. When her husband died, she stayed in the South and opened schools for freed slave children. During the 1890s, she wrote about her memories of the war. Hers is the only published book about the Civil War by an African-American woman.

8 AFTER THE WAR

After the battles of Gettysburg and Vicksburg in 1863, the tide turned against the Confederacy. The Confederate army was worn down. Their soldiers suffered shortages of food and supplies. Many soldiers felt hopeless and deserted the army.

General Lee (middle left) surrendered to General Grant (middle right) on April 9, 1865.

In April 1865, Union forces captured Richmond, Virginia, the Confederate capital. Soon after, Confederate General Robert E. Lee surrendered. Then other generals surrendered. The Civil War was finally over, and 4 million slaves were now free. But the peace came with a cost. Of the 3 million soldiers who fought in the war, about 620,000 had died.

The fighting had left much of the United States in shambles. All the damage caused during the war had to be repaired. Cities in the South needed to be rebuilt, and crops needed to be replanted.

But not everyone was interested in healing. Some people in the South remained angry about their loss. One of these men, John Wilkes Booth, **assassinated** President Lincoln just a few days after the Civil War ended. Despite the Union's success, it was years before freed slaves were treated as full citizens under the law.

President Lincoln was assassinated at Ford's Theatre on April 15, 1865.

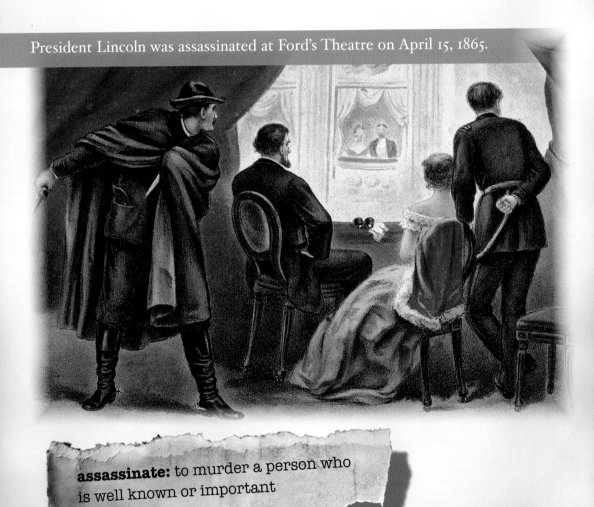

assassinate: to murder a person who is well known or important

GLOSSARY

amputation (am-pyuh-TAY-shun)—the removal of an arm or leg, usually because the part is damaged

artillery (ar-TI-luhr-ee)—cannons and other large guns used during battles

assassinate (us-SASS-uh-nate)—to murder a person who is well known or important

Confederate (kuhn-FED-ur-uht)—having to do with the 11 southern states that left the United States in 1860 and 1861 to form the Confederate States of America

engineer (en-juh-NEER)—someone who is trained to design and build bridges, roads, or other structures

infantry (IN-fuhn-tree)—a group of soldiers trained to fight and travel on foot

plantation (plan-TAY-shuhn)—a large farm where crops such as cotton, tobacco, and sugarcane are grown; before 1865, most plantations in the southern United States were run by slave labor

regiment (REJ-uh-muhnt)—a large group of soldiers who fight together as a unit; full regiments have about 1,000 soldiers, but most Civil War regiments were smaller

secede (si-SEED)—to formally withdraw from a group or an organization

Union (YOON-yuhn)—the states that remained loyal to the federal government during the Civil War

BIBLIOGRAPHY

Cotham Jr., Edward T., ed. *The Southern Journey of a Civil War Marine: The Illustrated Note-Book of Henry O. Gusley*. Austin, Texas: University of Texas Press, 2006.

Koonce, Donald B., ed. *Doctor to the Front: The Recollections of Confederate Surgeon Thomas Fanning Wood, 1861-1865*. Voices of the Civil War. Knoxville, Tenn.: University of Tennessee Press, 2000.

Malles, Ed, ed. *Bridge Building in Wartime: Colonel Wesley Brainerd's Memoir of the 50th New York Volunteer Engineers*. Voices of the Civil War. Knoxville, Tenn.: University of Tennessee Press, 1997.

Mosby, John S. *The Memoirs of Colonel John S. Mosby*. Southern Classics. Nashville, Tenn.: J.S. Sanders & Co., 1995.

Taylor, Susie King. *Reminiscences of My Life in Camp*. Athens, Ga.: University of Georgia Press, 2006.

Watkins, Sam R. *"Co. Aytch," Maury Grays, First Tennessee Regiment; Or, A Side Show of the Big Show*. Franklin, Tenn.: Providence House Publishers, 2007.

READ MORE

Doeden, Matt. *The Civil War: An Interactive History Adventure*. You Choose Books. Mankato, Minn., Capstone Press, 2010.

Landau, Elaine. *The Battle of Gettysburg: Would You Lead the Fight?* What Would You Do? Berkeley Heights, N.J.: Enslow Elementary, 2009.

Rebman, Renee C. *The Union Soldier*. We the People. Minneapolis: Compass Point Books, 2007.

INTERNET SITES

FactHound offers a safe, fun way to find Internet sites related to this book. All of the sites on FactHound have been researched by our staff.

Here's all you do:

Visit *www.facthound.com*

Type in this code: 9781429647366

INDEX